SOMEONE CARES

*Scripture Truths for
Those Who Are Ill*

Published by

South Holland, Illinois 60473, USA

Box 5037, Burlington, Ontario, L7R 3Y8, Canada

Box 464, Penrith, NSW 2751, Australia

Box 77-047, Mt. Albert, New Zealand

A100–18

For You

This booklet is given to you
as a gift.
We want you to keep it
so that you may read it again
during the course of your illness
and convalescence.
Perhaps others will also be able
to receive a blessing from it
as you share it with them.

May God strengthen you
as you read His Word
And grant you
peace of mind and heart
As you learn
to commit your ways
unto Him.

Listen

Sickness and weakness
*   bring with them*
*   all kinds of reactions—*
*   fear*
*   uncertainty*
*   loneliness*
*   hurt.*

The sick person
*   wonders what might happen to him,*
*   often fearing the worst,*
*   while still hoping for the best.*

While you are ill
*   or convalescing,*
We invite you to listen
*   to words of confidence and hope,*
Words given to you by God Himself
*   in the pages of the Bible.*

When you trust in God,
You may have
*   great confidence in the present and*
*   great hope for the future*
Because God loves you.

And God promises richly to supply
*   all your needs*
*   both for time and for eternity*
Through Christ Jesus.

God Understands

God knows all about
your present weakness and trial.
He knows what you are going through.
He understands your hurts
and your fears.
He has not forsaken you
or forgotten about you.

Jesus Christ, the Son of God,
went through great suffering Himself.
And it is He
who comes to strengthen
and to comfort you
in your affliction.

Listen to Him!

He understands!

The Bible Says. . .

Cast all your anxiety
   on him
Because he cares
   for you.
                    I Peter 5:7

Taste and see
   that the Lord is good;
Blessed is the man
   who takes refuge
      in him.
                    Psalm 34:8

The Lord is close
   to the brokenhearted
And saves those
   who are crushed in spirit.
                    Psalm 34:18

Because he [Jesus] himself suffered
   when he was tempted,
He is able to help those
   who are being tempted.
                    Hebrews 2:18

God's Love

When you fully trust
in God,
You know that God's love
will never fail you.
Nothing can separate you
from God's love.

Circumstances
may sometimes cause you
to feel forsaken,
But you never are.

You may temporarily fail
to enjoy the presence
and love of God
because of your hurts
or fears,
But God's love is still there!

Circumstances
don't change the reality
of God's presence and love,
Even though you may change
in your awareness
of them.

God remains lovingly faithful,
and faithfully loving.

God doesn't change!

The Bible Says. . .

You are kind and forgiving,
*   O Lord,*
Abounding in love to all
*   who call on you.*

                    Psalm 86:5

Who shall separate us
*   from the love of Christ?*
Shall trouble or hardship
*   or persecution or famine*
*   or nakedness or danger or sword?*
No, in all these things
*   we are more than conquerors*
*   through him who loved us.*
For I am convinced
*   that neither death nor life,*
*   neither angels nor demons,*
*   neither the present nor the future,*
*   nor any powers,*
Neither height nor depth,
*   nor anything else*
*   in all creation,*
Will be able to separate us
*   from the love of God*
*   that is in Christ Jesus*
*   our Lord.*

                    Romans 8:35, 37-39

Uncertainty

Perhaps you feel
    that God is punishing you
    for some wrong you have done.
You may feel
    that you deserve
    all the trials you are going through.

Is that how it is?

It is true
    that God does not always intervene
    to keep sickness away
    from His children.

But
    your sickness and your suffering
    can never pay for your sins.
Only Jesus Christ can do that.

It is by His sufferings,
    not yours,
That you are made right with God.

And remember,
    God can graciously use
    even your suffering and sickness
    for your ultimate good,
If you humbly and sincerely
    commit them
    unto Him.

The Bible Says. . .

A righteous man
    may have many troubles,
But the Lord delivers him
    from them all.

Psalm 34:19

And we know that
    in all things
God works for the good
    of those
    who love him.

Romans 8:28a

He [Jesus] was pierced
    for our transgressions,
He was crushed
    for our iniquities;
The punishment that brought
    us peace
    was upon him,
And by his wounds
    we are healed.

Isaiah 53:5

And my God will meet
    all your needs
According to his glorious riches
    in Christ Jesus.

Philippians 4:19

Jim Whitmer

He tends his flock
like a shepherd:
He gathers the lambs
in his arms
and carries them
close to his heart;
He gently leads those
that have young.

Isaiah 40:11

Trust

One of life's great blessings
is to have someone
you can trust.
Completely!
With everything!

Between you and
the one you trust
There is total openness,
complete confidence.
The one you trust
will never fail you
or leave you
No matter what happens.

God is Someone like that,
Someone you can trust.
He has promised
never to forget you
or to fail you.
He will not get weary
of listening to you.
He will not leave you
when your trials increase.

God wants to be your Friend.
He wants you to trust Him.
Completely!
With everything!

The Bible Says. . .

"Call upon me
in the day of trouble;
I will deliver you,
and you will honor me."
                                Psalm 50:15

When I am afraid,
I will trust in you.
In God, whose word I praise,
in God I trust;
I will not be afraid.
What can mortal man do
to me?
                                Psalm 56:3, 4

The Lord is my light
and my salvation—
Whom shall I fear?
                                Psalm 27:1

The Lord is a refuge
for the oppressed,
A stronghold
in times of trouble.
Those who know your name
will trust in you,
For you, Lord,
have never forsaken
those who seek you.
                                Psalm 9:9,10

Fear

Perhaps you are wondering
*   just how serious*
*   your illness is.*
You may be fearing the worst.
*   Or you may already know the worst.*
And that may make you afraid,
*   afraid of today,*
*   afraid of tomorrow,*
*   afraid of what will happen to you.*

Or you may be
*   afraid of what will happen*
*   to your loved ones*
*   if you don't make it,*
*   if you don't get better.*

Does God understand those fears?
Does He really care
*   when you're afraid?*

Of course He does.

That's why He promises
*   that He will never leave you.*
He assures you
*   that He will never forsake you,*
*   no matter how rough*
*   the way may be.*

Tomorrow may be uncertain,
*   but the promises of God are not.*
Do not let the fear of the unknown
*   take away the comfort*
*   of that which is sure!*

The Bible Says. . .

Be strong and courageous.
Do not be afraid
or terrified . . .
For the Lord your God
goes with you;
He will never leave you
nor forsake you.

Deuteronomy 31:6

The Lord is my shepherd.
I shall lack nothing.

He makes me lie down
in green pastures,
He leads me beside
quiet waters.

Even though I walk
through the valley
of the shadow
of death,
I will fear no evil,
for you are with me;
Your rod and your staff,
they comfort me.

Surely goodness and love
will follow me
all the days of my life,
And I will dwell
in the house of the Lord
forever.

Psalm 23:1, 2, 4, 6

But now,
  this is what the Lord says,
"Fear not,
  for I have redeemed you;
I have called you by name;
  you are mine.
When you pass through the waters,
  I will be with you;
And when you pass through
  the rivers,
    they will not
      sweep over you."

Isaiah 43:1, 2

Thankfulness

Many people find it easy to be thankful
when things go well,
But they find it hard to be thankful
when things go wrong.

They quickly forget
their years of good health
after a few days of illness.
They quickly forget
their years of freedom
after a few days of confinement.

And thankfulness drains away
along with
their declining
strength.

Do not lose your thankful spirit
when you lose your health.
God has not left you;
His love has not failed you.
God still wants the best for you,
no matter how little
you may understand that
right now.

Do not focus
on what you have lost.
Learn to give thanks
for what you have!

The Bible Says. . .

I will extol the Lord
   at all times;
His praise will always be
   on my lips.
My soul will boast in the Lord;
   let the afflicted hear
    and rejoice.
Glorify the Lord with me;
   let us exalt his name
    together.

Psalm 34:1-3

Though the fig tree
   does not bud
And there are no grapes
   on the vines,
Though the olive crop fails
   and the fields produce no food,
Though there are no sheep
   in the pen
    and no cattle
     in the stalls,
Yet I will rejoice
   in the Lord,
I will be joyful
   in God
    my Savior.

Habakkuk 3:17, 18

Discouragement

Hospitals and nursing homes
*   are great places to have around*
*   when you're in need.*
But they're not like home!

All the familiar things are gone,
*   your normal routine is interrupted,*
*   your favorite foods are not available,*
And someone you hardly know
*   tells you what you may*
*   and may not do.*
You feel so dreadfully out of place—
*   almost like a prisoner.*

You hurt,
*   you weep,*
*   nothing seems to go right.*
And you simply don't know
*   how long it will be*
*   before you are well again.*

God understands all of that,
*   and He wants you*
*   to be honest with Him.*
He doesn't want you to hide
*   how you really feel.*
He wants you to talk to Him
*   about it.*

He promises to listen!

The Bible Says. . .

As the deer pants
    for streams of water,
So my soul pants for you,
    O God.
My soul thirsts for God,
    for the living God.
Where can I go
    and meet with God?
My tears have been my food
    day and night,
While men say to me all day long,
    "Where is your God?"

Why are you downcast
    O my soul?
Why so disturbed within me?

Put your hope in God,
    for I will yet praise him,
        my Savior and my God.

By day the Lord directs his love,
    at night his song
        is with me—
A prayer to the God of my life.
            Psalm 42:1-3, 5, 8

Prayer

Praying is a precious privilege.

Through prayer
you may find relief
from anxiety and fear.
Through prayer
you may find fellowship with God
and enjoy a blessed peace.

But sometimes
you may be too sick to pray,
or too tired.
Or it may seem
that God isn't listening.
Or you hardly know
what to pray for.
What then?

Then it's good to know
that many others
are praying for you.
Loved ones, family, friends
are lifting you up
in prayer before God.

And Jesus Himself
continues to pray for you
in Heaven itself.
And the Holy Spirit, too,
who knows all your needs,
presents them perfectly
before your Father in Heaven.

The Bible Says. . .

Do not be anxious
about anything,
But in everything,
by prayer and petition,
with thanksgiving,
present your requests to God.
And the peace of God,
which transcends all understanding,
Will guard your hearts
and your minds
in Christ Jesus.

Philippians 4:6, 7

Let us then approach
the throne of grace
with confidence,
So that we may receive mercy
and find grace to help us
in our time of need.

Hebrews 4:16

Praise be to God,
who has not rejected my prayer
or withheld his love
from me!

Psalm 66:20

He will respond to the prayer
of the destitute;
He will not despise
their plea.

Psalm 102:17

O you
  who hear prayer,
    to you
      all men will come.

Psalm 65:2

Patience

For many people
life is so terribly busy.
Perhaps it is for you, too.
There simply isn't enough time
to do everything
you would like to do.

Then sickness comes.

And with it come
frustration and irritation,
Because you are no longer the master
of your own affairs.
You are simply no longer in control.
You need help.

Sickness, therefore, gives you
an opportunity to learn patience.
God Himself sometimes lovingly
slows you down a bit
from the frenzied pace
of your normal life.
He gives you the opportunity to look up,
to look up to Him,
to start talking with Him again,
to take a new look into His Word.

Patience! Don't be so restless!
Try to make the most
of this interruption
in your life.

Learn to wait upon the Lord!

The Bible Says. . .

I waited patiently
   for the Lord;
He turned to me
   and heard my cry.
He lifted me out of the slimy pit,
   out of the mud and mire;
He set my feet on a rock
   and gave me a firm place
      to stand.
He put a new song in my mouth,
   a hymn of praise
      to our God.
Many will see and fear
   and put their trust
      in the Lord.

Psalm 40:1-3

I know what it is
   to be in need,
And I know what it is
   to have plenty.
I have learned the secret
   of being content
      in any and every situation,
Whether well fed or hungry,
   whether living in plenty
      or in want.
I can do everything
   through him
      who gives me strength.

Philippians 4:12, 13

Loneliness

Some people are very lonely.
They do not have to learn patience.
Nothing ever seems to happen,
so they are never in a hurry.
They always wait.
And no one ever seems to come.

Maybe you are like that.
Or maybe
you are like that now.
You expected a lot of visitors,
but hardly anyone comes.
Or even if some do come,
there are still so many hours
when you are alone.

And it hurts
to be lonely.
It can hurt as much
as the sickness does.
And even a lot more!

God understands those hurts,
and He cares about them.
He wants to help you
in your loneliness.
He wants you to know Him
as a Friend.

There may still be times of loneliness
for you,
But if God is truly your Friend,
you will never
be alone.

The Bible Says. . .

"The Lord himself goes before you
   and will be with you;
He will never leave you
   nor forsake you.
Do not be afraid;
   do not be discouraged."

                  Deuteronomy 31:8

"Be strong and courageous.
   Do not be terrified;
      do not be discouraged,
For the Lord your God
   will be with you
      wherever you go."

                  Joshua 1:9

The Lord says,
   "He will call upon me,
     and I will answer him;
I will be with him in trouble,
    I will deliver him
      and honor him."

                  Psalm 91:15

"So do not fear,
   for I am with you;
Do not be dismayed,
   for I am your God.
I will strengthen you
   and will help you;
I will uphold you
   with my righteous right hand."

                  Isaiah 41:10

Graeme Johnstone

"Even to your old age
and gray hairs
I am he,
I am he
who will
sustain you.
I have made you
and I will
carry you;
I will sustain you
and I
will rescue
you."

Isaiah 46:4

Learning

Being sick
    is rarely enjoyable,
But it may give you an opportunity
    to learn some precious new truths,
    or to re-learn some old ones.

For example,

You may have forgotten
    just how much you depend on God—
    for everything!

Or perhaps
    you were starting to take
    your health and strength for granted.
You just assumed
    that you would always be well,
    that sickness would always be for others.

Or you may have been neglecting
    some very important things in your life—
        your relationship to your family,
            or to your friends,
                or to your God.

Or you may simply
    not have taken enough time
    to think about the meaning and purpose
    of your life.

And now you have
    the opportunity to think.

Illness is a time for learning!

The Bible Says. . .

Consider it pure joy, my brothers,
    whenever you face trials
        of many kinds,
Because you know
    that the testing of your faith
        develops perseverance.
Perseverance must finish its work
    so that you may be mature and complete,
        not lacking in anything.
                James 1:2-4

God disciplines us for our good,
    that we may share
        in his holiness.
No discipline seems pleasant at the time,
    but painful.
Later on, however,
    it produces a harvest
        of righteousness and peace
For those who have been trained by it.
                Hebrews 12:10b, 11

In this you greatly rejoice,
    though now for a little while
        you may have had to suffer grief
        in all kinds of trials.
These have come so that
    your faith . . . may be proved genuine
    and may result in
        praise, glory and honor
            when Christ is revealed.
                I Peter 1:6, 7

Confidence

Hope springs eternal
   in the heart
      of the child of God.

Nothing is ever hopeless
   when your ways are committed
      to your Heavenly Father.

God's power is unlimited;
   His goodness knows no measure;
      His mercy knows no end.

No matter what news
   the day may bring you, therefore,
You can accept it
   with quiet confidence.
For nothing whatever
   will happen to you
      beyond your Father's loving control.

Your Father
   constantly watches over you.
Not one hair of your head
   will fall to the ground
      without His will!

Your confidence for the future
   is built upon
   an unmovable foundation.

The Bible Says. . .

The Lord says,
    "Fear not,
      for I have redeemed you;
    I have called you by name;
    you are mine."
                    Isaiah 43:1b

Those who trust in the Lord
    are like Mount Zion
        which cannot be shaken
            but endures forever.
As the mountains surround Jerusalem,
    so the Lord surrounds his people
        both now
            and forevermore.
                    Psalm 125:1, 2

Jesus said,
    "Are not two sparrows
      sold for a penny?
    Yet not one of them
      will fall to the ground
        apart from the will
          of your Father.
    And even the hairs
      of your head
        are all numbered.
    So don't be afraid;
    you are worth more
      than many sparrows."
                    Matthew 10:29-31

Melanie Jongsma

*I can do everything
through him
who gives
me strength.*

Philippians 4:13

Healing

God has made you
    in such a wonderful way
        that your sick and tired body
           often restores itself.

Sometimes God heals you
    through the use of medicine,
        or through surgery,
           or through special treatment.

Sometimes God heals you directly
    in answer to special prayer.

However it may happen
    that you get well,
It is God
    who is the Great Physician.

So when you are well again,
    and when you give thanks
        to all who have helped you
           during your time of illness,

Remember
    to thank the Great Physician
        first of all—
           and above all!

And then use your healed body
    joyfully
        to serve the Lord!

The Bible Says. . .

It is good to praise the Lord
    and make music
        to your name,
           O Most High,
To proclaim your love
    in the morning
And your faithfulness
    at night . . . .
For you make me glad
    by your deeds,
        O Lord;
I sing for joy
    at the works
        of your hands.

                Psalm 92:1, 2, 4

He gives strength
    to the weary
And increases the power
    of the weak.
Even youths grow tired and weary,
    and young men
        stumble and fall;
But those who hope in the Lord
    will renew their strength.
They will soar on wings
    like eagles;
They will run
    and not grow weary,
They will walk
    and not be faint.

                Isaiah 40:29-31

Comfort

Someone once wrote:

My only comfort,
both in life and in death,
Is that I am not my own,
but belong with body and soul
to my faithful Savior, Jesus Christ.

If you are able to say that,
then no matter what happens,
you can rest in peace.

Whether you get well quickly
or slowly,
Whether you get well completely
or only in part,
Or even whether or not
you get well at all,
You will be at peace with God.

To belong to Jesus Christ
is to be a child of God.
To be a child of God
is to be accepted by God,
to be forgiven by God,
to be loved by God.

That is comfort!

The Bible Says. . .

Jesus said,
    "Peace I leave with you;
        my peace I give you.
    I do not give to you
        as the world gives.
    Do not let your hearts be troubled
        and do not be
            afraid."

                    John 14:27

Jesus said,
    "I have told you these things,
        so that in me
            you may have peace.
    In this world
        you will have trouble.
    But take heart!
        I have overcome the world."
                    John 16:33

You [God] will keep
    in perfect peace
    him whose mind
        is steadfast,
Because he trusts in you.

                    Isaiah 26:3

Invitation

Throughout this booklet
*   we have been assuming that*
*   you are a child of God.*

Some of you, however,
*   may not yet have come*
*   to know Christ personally.*
You know that you are not yet
*   at peace with God.*
But you would very much like to be.

You very much want the blessings
*   of comfort*
*   and assurance*
*   and peace*
Which are described in these pages.

God invites you to receive them!

Accept that gracious invitation
*   by praying the following prayer*
*   or a similar prayer of your own.*

Father,
*   I humbly come to You in Jesus' name,*
*   asking You to fill my longing heart.*
*   Please take away all my sins,*
*   and fill my life*
*   with Your love and peace.*
*   I trust You to do this*
*   because of what Jesus did for me*
*   when He suffered and died*
*   and rose again.*
*   I pray in Jesus' name. Amen.*

The Bible Says. . .

Jesus said,
"I tell you the truth,
whoever hears my Word
and believes him who sent me
has eternal life
and will not be condemned;
He has crossed over
from death to life."

John 5:24

Jesus said,
"Come to me,
all you who are weary
and burdened,
And I will give you
rest."

Matthew 11:28

To all who received him [Jesus],
to those who believed
in his name,
He gave the right
to become children
of God.

John 1:12

I will lie down
  and sleep in peace,
For you alone,
  O Lord,
Make me dwell
  in safety.

Psalm 4:8

This booklet has been given to you by

If you are not already involved
in the worship and fellowship
of a Bible-believing church,
we invite you
to write or call us.
We will be happy to help you.